Time and Space in the Novels of Samuel Richardson

by

JOHN SAMUEL BULLEN
Associate Professor of English

29576

UTAH STATE UNIVERSITY PRESS

LOGAN, UTAH

MONOGRAPH SERIES

| Volume XII | July, 1965 | Number 2 |

Editor

Milton C. Abrams, Librarian

Associate Editors

Austin E. Fife, Professor of Languages
M. Judd Harmon, Professor of Political Science
S. George Ellsworth, Professor of History
John M. Patrick, Professor of English
Eldon J. Gardner, Professor of Zoology and Dean of the
College of Science

Requests for copies should be addressed to

Public Services and Information

Utah State University, Logan

Table of Contents

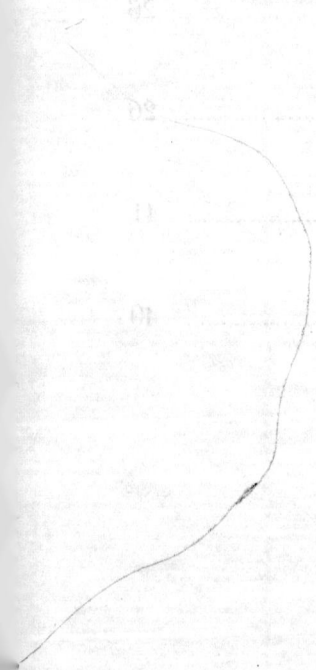

Introduction

In its broader evaluations, critical opinion of the works of Samuel Richardson has remained almost constant for many years. Baldly stated, the standard judgment in our time is that *Pamela* is a novel with slight intrinsic but great historic value; that *Clarissa* is a masterpiece, qualified to stand with the great works of fiction of all time; and that *Sir Charles Grandison* is an unredeemable bore, important only for the influence it had on later novelists, most notably Jane Austen. With this classification of the canon I have no quarrel, and I attempt, in the present study, neither to promote wider critical acceptance of Richardson's first and last novels, nor to reduce the regard for his second. If ever accomplished, those changes will result from the altered tastes of future readers.

My study arises from a belief that not everything has been said about Richardson that can be said or that needs to be said. In spite of my acceptance of prevailing judgments, I do not believe that one can legitimately regard Richardson's contribution as a solidified fact of literary history, any more than one can pigeonhole Shakespeare. If nothing else, Richardson provides too much bulk to be classified conveniently. As much as any novelist, he defeats the reader's attempt to achieve the ideal critical effort described by Percy Lubbock: "To grasp the shadowy and fantasmal form of a book, to hold it fast, to turn it over and survey it at leisure." [1] There is so much to a Richardson novel that just when one is satisfied at having grasped it, out from the side, like a bubble of dough, oozes a new area for consideration. The ultimate reading of Richardson will not, and should not, ever be reached.

Richardson's value lies chiefly, I believe, in what he is able to demonstrate about the impulse of the modern world to write novels and to read them. Long on flaws, and equally long on virtues, Richardson is a sourcebook for much that has gone into the novel since his time. Though I make no attempt, in this study, to treat Richard-

---

[1] *The Craft of Fiction* (London, 1921), p. 1.

son as an influence on later novelists, I operate on the assumption that he accomplished something that had not been accomplished before and that he started a type of literary endeavor that has endured since. Unquestionably, I believe, such a writer deserves repeated study.

I have focused this study of Richardson on his handling of time and space, because here, I believe, one finds him relatively undistracted by his didactic concerns and able to operate more genuinely as a novelist. These aspects of his procedure, moreover, have generally received slight attention from critics, who largely emphasize his handling of character. Arthur Sherbo, an exception to this tendency, has demonstrated that while Richardson fostered an acceptance of his novels as "real-life stories," he at the same time made it impossible for his readers to identify the actual times, places, and persons with which his novels were supposed to be concerned. He created, in Sherbo's words, "a realistic yet sufficiently vague background of reference," [2] thus implying that the author, if he chose, could supply the actual date of each event and specify its location. But it is not the relationship between the events of the novels and the external calendars and maps of history that I wish to examine here. I wish rather to describe how Richardson — who, after all, knew that he was not offering genuine letters to the public — employed various principles of time and space in creating the fictional worlds of his novels.

---

[2] "Time and Place in Richardson's *Clarissa*," *Boston University Studies in English*, III (1957), 143.

I. Time in *Pamela*

The location of narrative within fixed and specified limits of time, and, further, the employment of time (its duration, its relativity, its apparent absence) in various significant ways in the development of a fictional world — these have become common procedures in the novel since Richardson. On a novel's attention to relationships in time depends the power of probability in its characters and actions; yet a novel's sequence of time draws its significance from actualized elements that are shown to exist within it. On the one hand, as Ian Watt observes, "the novel's closeness to the texture of daily experience directly depends upon the employment of a much more minutely discriminated time-scale than had previously been employed in narrative." [3] The reader's sense that within the experience of the novel time has passed, is passing, and will pass, just as it does in life, gives him the terms for dealing with the novel's contents as physically present in a temporal continuum. This is true even when a novel's time-scheme is distorted and its chronology jumbled, for the distortion must assume a normal pattern of passing time. On the other hand, as Hans Meyerhoff observes, time "is meaningful only within the . . . context of personal experience, not within the context of nature." [4] The reader's acceptance that characters and events might exist or might have existed gives relevance to his observation of the time process. Thus, in the full dimension of a novel, time, character, and event are mutually dependent, infusing one another with the particularity that negotiates the novel's realism.

It is instructive to observe that two of the early novelists, Defoe and Richardson, happened to select modes of narration that place natural emphasis on units of time. The autobiographical memoir of Defoe effectually sets limits on the duration of experience, whether

---

[3] *The Rise of the Novel* (Berkeley, 1957), p. 22. Watt develops a clear analysis of the concepts of time and their employment in literature from Greece and Rome through the Renaissance in contrast to the specific use of time in the novel (pp. 21-24).

[4] *Time in Literature* (Berkeley, 1955), p. 28.

a lifetime or a period of years. Moreover, within the span of the memoir, the sequential nature of the events is emphasized by their having started at a fixed point that implies movement through time toward a point of termination. Even when, as is often the case in Defoe's work, the time relationship of one event to another is casual rather than specific, the intimation of chronology is retained. The epistolary mode of Richardson is likewise conducive to the portrayal of temporal units. The very notion of a letter carries with it the idea of a specific moment of composition that in turn establishes for the subject matter a position in time. Although the epistolary technique, unlike the autobiographical memoir, does not in itself suggest clearly demarked points of beginning and ending for the total block of experience presented, it nevertheless can function, perhaps more effectively than the memoir, on the smaller scale of day-by-day, or minute-by-minute, transcription of time relationships. In the memoir, time can be confined; in the letter, it can be domesticated.

Richardson, however, did not particularize time elements simply as a matter of course, even though the form in which he wrote lends itself so easily to an almost automatic accounting for days and weeks. In *Pamela,* he appears to have learned almost in the process of writing that attention to time gave greater weight to the other details of his novel. The early letters of Pamela to her parents, for example, bear no label of day, time, or place, epistolary elements that are scrupulously attended to through most of the rest of Richardson's work. Nor do Pamela's early letters carry much internal concern with time or with the placement of events in time relationships. In her first letter, Pamela announces the death of her lady, but does not say when the death occurred; by the twentieth letter, we are amazed to learn that fourteen months have elapsed "since my lady's death" (I, 41),[5] for we are still involved in the preliminary stages of B.'s forays against Pamela. Other time relationships are equally vague in the early sections. Pamela reveals in her fourth letter that Lady Davers "has been a month at our house" (I, 6),

---

[5] In this study, all citations refer to *The Novels of Samuel Richardson,* with a Life of the Author and Introductions by W. L. Phelps. 19 vols. (New York, 1901-02). In this edition, *Pamela* appears in four volumes, *Clarissa* in eight, and *Sir Charles Grandison* in seven. Citations, most of which will appear parenthetically in the text, will include the volume number of the particular novel, not of the entire set.

though nothing else has indicated the passage of this much time in Pamela's own experience. Even events that are crucial to Pamela's situation are located hazily: "[O]ne day he came to me, as I was in the summer-house" (I, 14). Not "last Wednesday," but "one day." Within certain scenes, which themselves are obscurely placed in time, Pamela's account does begin to suggest the ticking of the clock: "Well, you may believe how uneasily I passed the time until his appointed hour came. Every minute, as it grew nearer, my terrors increased" (I, 27). But not until Pamela is confined at the Lincolnshire estate and begins to keep a journal does she start a methodical calendarizing of her narrative: "I am now come to Monday, the 5th day of my bondage and misery" (I, 125). From this point, in fact, to the end of *Pamela I*, her communications are dated at least with the weekday of composition, so that the rhythm of the narrative comes to be somewhat governed by the passage of time. The lack, however, of an overall structure of time for the novel tends to isolate the Lincolnshire section as an independent unit.

One could, of course, advance the supposition that Richardson's shift, after the first hundred pages of his novel, from a generalized to a particularized treatment of time was deliberate. It would be difficult, however, to support such a theory by citing advantages that he might consciously have hoped to gain from such a maneuver. It seems more likely that the change resulted from Richardson's recognition that as Pamela's predicament became increasingly specialized it demanded a more open acknowledgement of the consciousness of time that she would have in the circumstances, and, consequently, required a more tightly controlled time sequence than he had presented in the earlier passages. Whatever the cause, the consequence of the change is apparent, both in the increased vividness of scene and character after Pamela's arrival at the Lincolnshire estate and in the strengthened suggestion of a situation that undergoes complications and reaches its solution over a passage of time.[6] The world of the early sections of *Pamela* is almost as timeless as the world of

---

[6] Slightly less than two months pass between Pamela's arrival at the Lincolnshire estate and her marriage to B., but practically every day of the period is accounted for. In contrast, the preceding period, which seems much shorter, apparently covers more than a year. It is impossible, however, to determine the length of time covered by the early period with any accuracy.

The Pilgrim's Progress or *Euphues*. And in this timeless world, the case of Pamela seems almost as hypothetical as the situations in Richardson's own *Familiar Letters*. It may well be that the change we observe after the first hundred pages of *Pamela* shows the English novel coming to its first struggle with the patterns of experienced time.

If, during the writing of *Pamela I*, Richardson learned the value of closely observed time relationships, he did not immediately apply his lesson to his work, for in *Pamela II* he returns to a timeless world. He creates, in fact, a world in which almost no acknowledgement is made of the calendar or the clock. Only in two sections of the sequel do we find Pamela attaching distinct labels to her letters. In the first of these, Pamela sends what amounts to a running account of her social schedule to Polly Darnford. Although the various entries are headed, as in a journal, with Mondays and Tuesdays, such identifications have no real temporal kinship with the content of the letters, which typically summarize conversations but present no action. An entry headed "Saturday morning," for example, begins in the following way: "The countess being a little indisposed, Lady Davers and I took an airing this morning in the chariot, and had a great deal of discourse together" (III, 143). The great deal of discourse follows militantly. Thus, the time references could be eliminated entirely without altering the function of these letters. The second section that employs time references occurs, interestingly enough, during the only part of *Pamela II* that generates anything resembling a plot situation. After the surface of her marriage has been slightly rippled by B.'s extra-marital interest, Pamela, filled with suspense, writes a few notes to Lady Davers that tick off the hours until the reconciliation; she almost automatically falls back into the breathless manner of her pursued past: "I have only time to tell your ladyship (for the postman waits) that Mr. B. — has just come in" (IV, 113). When the doubts are lifted, the letters return to the miscellaneous treatises and leave time behind. The fact, therefore, that *Pamela II* is not regulated by a consistent time system is a contributing cause to its major flaw, the disjunction between narrative and non-narrative elements, a flaw that does not reappear in Richardson's work until *Sir Charles Grandison*. This gap is more noticeable in the sequel than in the original novel, probably because of the relatively thin line of action onto which is basted a disproportionate amount of discursive material. But even in a moderate amount this material would seem gratuitous, for it has no temporal connection with a continuity of events and therefore has no point of reference.

In *Pamela*, then, we see an unsure treatment of time that further reveals the tentative nature of Richardson's narrative powers at this point in his career. We see that the weakness of time in *Pamela* results not so much from an inherent defect in the narrative system itself as from Richardson's own inability to fuse, within the functioning of that system, his disparate attempts to present Pamela as both an individual girl at her moment in time and as a timeless example. More likely, the weakness results from Richardson's failure even to recognize that such a fusion is artistically desirable. Thus, the sections of *Pamela I* that do operate in particularized time seem the accidental results of Richardson's yielding to the demands of his narrative method rather than controlling it, a supposition that is further supported by the sole example of situational time in *Pamela II*. To observe a more successful and purposeful handling of time we must turn our attention to *Clarissa*.

II. Time in *Clarissa*

The detailed attention to time in *Clarissa* seems almost exces-
sive when contrasted to the paucity of time references in *Pamela*.
Between January 10, when Anna Howe writes to Clarissa requesting
the particulars of her situation, and December 18, when F. J. de la
Tour sends Belford a description of Lovelace's death, practically
every day is accounted for. During the months preceding Clarissa's
death in September, almost every hour is chronicled. With few
exceptions the letters carry identifying tags of day, date, and often
very hour of composition. Moreover, the letters are packed with time
references: "just now," "last night," "about six," "this morning early."
The fastidious concern with time reveals a Richardson who has consciously organized a set of circumstances within a highly particularized temporal unit. What then, are the results in *Clarissa* of the
close regard for time?

From the opening pages of *Clarissa* the characters and events
reveal a particularity that contrasts markedly with the hypothetical
quality early in *Pamela*. Clarissa's first few letters supply expository
material in response to Anna's request for "the whole of your story
from the time that Mr. Lovelace was first introduced into your
family" (I, 3), thus providing an immediate context of time relationships from which the opening situation can develop. Once under-
way, events, character, and time supply further meaning and particularity to one another. The antipathy of the Harlowes toward Lovelace, for example, is made explicit by the detailed tracing through
time of his contacts with members of the family. This in turn sets
up the expectancy of future consequences, so that the entire chain of
events gains significance from and grants importance to the time
sequence. Thus, passages such as the following not only depict a
present moment, but also reverberate with the implications of past
and future events. Clarissa is explaining to Anna that Lovelace
surprised her near the woodhouse at Harlowe Place:

> I had hitherto, as you know, kept him at a distance: and now,
> as I recovered myself, judge of my first emotions, when I recollected

his character from every mouth of my family; his enterprising temper; and found myself alone with him, in a place so near a bye-lane, and so remote from the house.

But his respectful behaviour soon dissipated these fears, and gave me others; lest we should be seen together, and information of it given to my brother: the consequences of which, I could readily think, would be, if not further mischief, an imputed assignation, a stricter confinement, a forfeited correspondence with you, my beloved friend, and a pretence for the most violent compulsion: and neither the one set of reflections, nor the other, acquitted him to me for his bold intrusion (I, 215).

The passage places in time the reactions of the startled Clarissa, so that the encounter is a very real one; but it also expands the progression of events with further layers of significance. Later passages in the novel perform similar functions, but rest on a broader time-experience base and point to an increasingly narrow termination. Following Clarissa's second escape from Mrs. Sinclair's house, for example, Lovelace writes Belford that she has been arrested and confined in the house of a sheriff's officer:

Hasten, hasten, dear Jack; for the love of God, hasten to the injured charmer! my heart bleeds for her! — she deserved not this! — I dare not stir. It will be thought done by my contrivance — and if I am absent from this place, that will confirm the suspicion.

Damnation seize quick this accursed woman [Mrs. Sinclair]! — Yet she thinks she has made no small merit with me. Unhappy, thrice unhappy circumstances! — At a time too, when better prospects were opening for the sweet creature!

Hasten to her! — Clear me of this cursed job. Most sincerely, by all that's sacred, I swear you may! — Yet have I been such a villainous plotter, that the charming sufferer will hardly believe it: although the proceeding be so dirtily low.

Set her free the moment you see her: without conditioning, free! — On your knees, for me, beg her pardon: and assure her, that wherever she goes, I will not molest her: no, nor come near her without her leave: and be sure allow not any of the d----d crew to go near her — only let her permit *you* to receive her commands from time to time. — You have always been her friend and advocate. What would I now give, had I permitted you to have been a successful one! (VI, 229-230).

The intensity of Lovelace's language gains its effect not only from the situation that he faces, but from the continuity of everything that has gone before with everything that is to come. The processes of time have now impounded every aspect of the novel and there is no escape.

The detailed time scheme of *Clarissa,* then, permits the narrative to advance with individualized realism and with increasing significance. But it also has considerable effect on the non-narrative intentions of the novel. Whereas in *Pamela II* the lack of a regulated time scheme frequently emphasizes the isolation of reflective, discursive, or analytical passages from their context, such material in *Clarissa* usually retains its pertinence primarily because it is fixed to time. Since the framework of dated correspondence provides a continuous time reference, the narrative can readily yield to other types of material without damage to the unity of the whole. This allows Richardson considerable freedom in varying the rhythm of the novel, for scenes of rapid or intense action can be preceded or followed by more leisurely sections. For example, after Clarissa's departure from Harlowe Place with Lovelace, her problems, while not yet particularly critical, are nevertheless perplexing. Has she made a mistake? Can she trust Lovelace? Her correspondence with Anna, therefore, can become something of a debate, a generalized discussion of honor, pride, modesty, honesty, the success of marriages, the behavior of parents, and the duty of children (III, 177-207, *passim*). Meantime, Lovelace reviews his success for Belford and reveals his further stratagems for removing Clarissa to London. After the calm, the tension begins to mount again at the arrival at Mrs. Sinclair's residence. The tendency of Clarissa to moralize, of Lovelace to gloat and justify, of Anna Howe to remonstrate, of all of them to generalize, can be employed in the pacing of events, thus helping to give *Clarissa* its monumental quality of the flux of life.

The fixed time sequence further contributes to the novel's rhythms by allowing breaks in the chronology. Under the conventions of the epistolary mode, the natural ordering of events is the chronological, and, of course, compared with Sterne's *Tristram Shandy* and later novels that experiment with juggled time patterns, Richardson's works all fairly consistently calendarize the outline of the action. Within the established framework, however, some flexibility is possible, and *Clarissa* reveals that Richardson is as enterprising in the timing of his material as he is in varying its type. The most frequently noted example of the effect created by delayed narration is Clarissa's account to Anna of the rape, her version following Lovelace's announcement of his triumph by over two hundred pages, and, in the time scheme, being written over three weeks after the event itself. The postponement is not simply a device to heighten the reader's suspense, although it admirably achieves that aim. Its primary effect is to give full weight to the physical and spiritual results that are produced in Clarissa by the violation and its attendant circumstances, and hence to prepare the way solidly for the denouement. The double view of the novel's situations is frequently provided by allowing a pause in one narrator's version to be filled by another view of the same period of time. Richardson is usually careful, when two characters cover the same ground, to give a new slant to the second account. Thus, Richardson introduces a series of letters by Lovelace: "Mr. Lovelace . . . gives an account to his friend (pretty much to the same effect with the lady's) of all that passed between them at the inns, in the journey, and till their fixing at Mrs. Sorling's; to avoid repetition, those passages in his narrative are extracted, which will serve to embellish hers; to open his views; or to display the humorous talent he was noted for" (III, 50). The rigidity of the temporal framework, then, allows considerable fluidity in both the timing and emphasis of the material that is placed within it. With the simple expedient of the dated letter, Richardson is able to delay, to move backward, to give parallel or contrasting versions, to extract, in other words, a maximum of significance from the fact that his characters and their actions operate in a flow of time that links the novel to life. If he does not explore all the potentials of rearranged time that we have seen handled in novels since, it is not because he had not discovered the significance of time in human experience. In his use of meaningful deviations from chronology, Richardson in *Clarissa* equipped the English novel with one of its most valuable procedures.

But the emphasis on time in *Clarissa* reveals more than a detailed schedule of events and consequences. It carries more significance than skillful manipulation of materials within a preconceived framework. For if time is stressed by the methods of the novel — in the creation of particularized incidents and in the establishment of varied rhythms — time is equally important as an inseparable part of the novel's matter, the pulses of external pressure and internal

motive that give *Clarissa* its dramatic inevitability. In a pervasive
yet subtle way, time operates throughout the novel as a major antagonist, inflexible and impartial, a cause and a consequence. The creation of this shaping and unifying structure of time is one of Richardson's masterly achievements. A novel of *Clarissa's* length and
methodical procedure, particularly one that focuses on a relatively
short span of action, might suggest a treatment of rather leisurely
affairs, yet through most of *Clarissa* we get a sense of urgency and
haste rather than deliberateness. Almost all important decisions are
made by the characters when they are under the pressure of time.
Even in the early stages, when it is primarily delivering exposition
and establishing initial motive, the novel presents situational crises
that result from the urgency of time. In answering charges "that
the story moved too slowly, particularly in the first and second volumes," Richardson defended the material as "the foundation of the
whole, and therefore a necessary part of the work" (*Clarissa*, Post-
script); but he might equally have answered that while the material
is lengthy and systematic, it does not deal with calm or unhurried
people and events. In Lovelace's brief courtship of Arabella, for
example, we see Lovelace taking full advantage of delay as a form
of pressure to force Arabella's refusal of his offer. First he pretends
diffidence, causing her some concern, for it is "right, surely, that
a woman should be put out of doubt *early* as to a man's intentions
in such a case as this" (I, 8); then he fertilizes her impatience by
continued silence: the "distant behavior, she must take it upon her
to say, was the more extraordinary as he continued his visits"
(*Ibid.*). Finally, he has "wrought her up to such a pitch of displeas-
ure with him, that it was impossible for her to recover herself at
the instant. Nevertheless he re-urged his question, as expecting a
definitive answer, without waiting for the return of her temper, or
endeavoring to mollify her; so that she was under a necessity of per-
sisting in her denial" (I, 9). Thus the clamps of time create a position from which Arabella cannot retreat. Clarissa's brother is likewise shown to act under the pressure of time: "The moment Mr.
Lovelace's visits were mentioned to him, he, without either hesita-
tion or apology, expressed his disapprobation of them" (I, 17). His
antipathy toward Lovelace is fully ignited when economic impera-
tives in the form of Solmes make action necessary. Thus he goads
Lovelace to the duel that establishes the armed camps. Clarissa indi-

cates the result: "My brother was disarmed, as you have heard; and on being brought home, and giving us ground to suppose he was much worse hurt than he really was, and a fever ensuing, every one flamed out; and all was laid at my door" (I, 23). Now the pressure turns to Clarissa herself, who never quite has time to resolve one situation before another is forced upon her, so that she becomes engaged in a battle with time that leads to her escape with Lovelace and to the pressures that lie beyond.

The opening sections of *Clarissa*, then, set up a strong bond between time and action. Time forces; time delays; time denies. The plot alters its direction with each shift in the heavy ballast of time that it carries. The characters, forced by the unerring compulsion of time, act impulsively on the basis of incomplete knowledge or incorrectly inferred facts. Even Lovelace, who is himself a manipulator and who often employs or increases the tensions of time for his own purposes, is prey to the grinding of the hours. Thus, when his scheme to trick Clarissa into marriage by means of the false Tomlinson appears to go awry, he confesses to Belford: "My divine Clarissa has puzzled me, and beat me out of my play: at one time I hope to overcome by *intimidating* her; at another, by *love;* by the amorous *see-saw,* as I have called it. And I have only now to join *surprise* to the other two, and see what can be done by all three" (V, 4). The fire in the upper chambers and Lovelace's consequent encounter with the half-dressed Clarissa bring further delays:

> But not to see her for a week! — Dear, pretty soul! how she anticipates me in everything! The counsellor will have finished the writings to-day or to-morrow, at furthest; the license with the parson, or the parson with the license, must also be procured within the next four-and-twenty hours; Pritchard is as good as ready with his indentures tripartite: Tomlinson is at hand with a favourable answer from her uncle — yet *not to see her for a week!* — Dear, sweet soul; — her good angel is gone a journey: is truanting at least. But nevertheless, in thy week's time, or in my less, my charmer, I doubt not to complete my triumph! (V, 26-27).

Clarissa manages her escape, and Lovelace is unhinged: *"Oh, for a curse to kill with!* — Ruined! Undone! Outwitted! Tricked! — Zounds, man, the lady has gone off! — Absolutely gone off! Escaped! —" (V, 35). Clarissa is found, and once again Lovelace is catapulted to action: "[M]idnight as it is, I have sent for a Blunt's chariot, to attend me here by day peep, with *my usual coachman,* if possible; and

knowing not what else to do with myself, I sat down, and in the joy
of my heart, have not only written thus far, but have concluded
upon the measures I shall take when admitted to her presence; for
well am I aware of the difficulties I shall have to contend with from
her perverseness" (V, 73). His recapture of Clarissa leads to the
rape, and Belford's letter of recrimination to Lovelace begins, interestingly enough, in temporal terms: "Oh, thou savage-hearted mon-
ster! What work hast thou made in *one guilty hour,* for a *whole age*
of repentance!" (V. 286). Lovelace demonstrably operates with a
greater consciousness of the effect of time than the other characters;
moreover, he is commonly the instigator of circumstances; hence, his
actions tend to result from more reflection than is observable in the
other characters. Nevertheless, in a good many of his significant acts
he is responding rapidly to the demands of the moment and placing
his trust in the oncoming hours and days to bring him the results he
wants.

Perhaps the most subtle and impressive evidence of time's dom-
ination is revealed in the gradually accelerated influence that it
has on Clarissa's mental and spiritual state. From the beginning,
Clarissa is subjected to disquieting situations, rapidly timed to establish for her a perpetually untenable position, for she never, during
the first two-thirds of the novel, quite understands the full implications of her situation. Initially, the main shocks to her mental state
are caused by personalities and situations: "This man, this Lovelace,
gives me great uneasiness. He is extremely bold and rash. He was
this afternoon at our church" (I, 173). Her confusion is nourished
by such external issues, but gradually a sense of time enters her
analyses of personality and circumstance:

> On what a point of time may one's worldly happiness depend!
> Had I but two hours more to consider of the matter . . . − but even
> then, perhaps, I might have given him a meeting. − Fool that I was!
> what had I to do to give him hope that I would *personally* acquaint
> him with the reason for my change of mind, if I did change it? II,
> 311).

This reflection is made as Clarissa recalls her nervous attempt to
decide between remaining in the garden to confront Lovelace or
avoiding the encounter to face the issue of Solmes, which her family
expects to settle on the following day. The passage clearly shows the

ambivalence into which Clarissa's mental processes are forced during the first stages of her situation. She herself becomes aware of the cloudiness of her judgment:

> I am strangely at a loss what to think of this man. He is a perfect Proteus. I can but write according to the shape he assumes at the time. Don't think *me* the changeable person, I beseech you, if in one letter I contradict what I wrote in another; nay, if I seem to contradict what I said in the same letter: for he is a perfect camelion. . . .
>
> Before I could finish my last to you, he sent up twice more to beg admittance. I returned for answer that I would see him at my own time: I would neither be invaded nor prescribed to (III, 136).

Increasingly Clarissa sees the temporal nature of her dilemma. Thus, after receiving Lovelace's written proposal of settlements, she laments to Anna:

> You see, my dear, what he offers. You see it is all my fault, that he has not made these offers before. I am a strange creature! — to be to blame in *everything*, and to *everybody;* yet neither intend the ill at the time, nor know it to be the ill [until] too late, or so nearly too late, that I must give up all the delicacy he talks of, to compound for my fault! (IV, 98-99).

But during the final stages of the story, Clarissa's consciousness of the encroachment of time becomes overwhelming, for the unavoidability of her death adds the dimension of finality to her every action. Thus Belford notes for Lovelace the observable signs of her physical decline as she prepares herself for death, being, for the first time, in full control of the circumstances of her existence: "having, as she had reason to think, but a short time and much to do in it, she must be a good housewife of her hours" (VII, 5). Her concern with time becomes obsessive and pervades her correspondence through the final volumes, as in the famous note to Lovelace in which she explains that she is about to leave for her father's house: "I am so taken up with my preparation for this joyful and long-wished-for journey, that I cannot spare one moment for other business, having several matters of the last importance to settle first" (VII, 226). Only in her last hours, with the pressure of time relieved, does her sense of urgency leave her: "I have left nothing to these last incapacitating hours. Nothing either to say or to do — and I bless God I have not. If I *had,* how unhappy should I be!" (VIII, 88). Clarissa sees her life in terms of its units of time, the past period of happiness contrasting with the present period of misery. She speaks, for example, of the impossibility of procuring "a sponge that will wipe out from the year the past fatal four months of my life" (VII, 72), and she pleads with her parents "to pronounce me blest and forgiven, since you will thereby sprinkle comfort through [my] last hours" (VII, 141). Mortal time comes to be considered by Clarissa as gaining its significance by proximity to the eternal time into which she will enter. Thus her spiritual concerns are intensified by the context of stress and counterstress between the material, temporary world she is leaving (the world of Lovelaces and Harlowes) and the unlimited, untimed world she looks to (the world of pure virtue, uninhibited by physical body). Lovelace's belief that "were she sure she should live but a day, she ought to die a wife" (VII, 144) draws her response that "were I to live more years than perhaps I may weeks, and there were not another man in the world, I could not, I would not, be yours" (VII, 159), a response resulting not so much from her distaste for Lovelace as from her almost complete disengagement from the world of time that he represents. Belford comprehends the thoroughness of the cleavage when he forbids Lovelace to "invade her in her last hours; since she must be extremely discomposed at such an interview; and it might make her leave the world the sooner for it" (VIII, 57). Clarissa presses the physician to indicate how long she has remaining: "Ten days? – a week? – How long sir?" (VII, 253), and looks to the end with an unambiguous eagerness that she has not granted to a single previous experience. Her comments to those who attend her final days have, consequently, a powerful quality of achieved realism that transcends the conventional nature of her observations:

> I am thinking . . . what a gradual and happy death God Almighty (blessed be His name) affords me! Who would have thought, that, suffering what I have suffered, and abandoned as I have been, with such a tender education as I have had, I should be so long a dying! – But see how by little and little it has come to this. I was first taken off from the power of *walking*: then I took a *coach* – a coach grew too violent an exercise: then I took a *chair* – the prison was a large DEATH-STRIDE upon me – I should have *suffered longer else!* – Next, I was unable to go to *church;* then to go *up* or *down stairs;* now hardly can move from one *room* to *another*: and a *less room* will soon hold me. – My *eyes* begin to fail me, so that at times I cannot see to read distinctly; and now I can hardly *write*, or hold a pen. – Next, I presume, I shall know nobody, nor be able to thank any of

you. . . And thus by little and little, in such a gradual sensible death as I am blessed with, God *dies away in us,* as I may say, all human satisfaction, in order to subdue His poor creatures to Himself. . . . This is a poor transitory life in its best enjoyments. We flutter about here and there, with all our vanities about us, like painted butterflies, for a gay, but very short season, till at last we lay ourselves down in a quiescent state, and turn into vile worms. And who knows in what form, or to what condition, we shall rise again? (VIII, 46-47).

The movement of this speech from the chronology of her progressive weakness to the spiritual implications that generalize her significance is parallel to her whole journey from time to eternity. Whatever answer we may choose to provide to the final question of her speech, we cannot fail to respond to the enormous weight of meaning that accrues through her encounter with time.

Clarissa is Richardson's most successful treatment of time. It is a novel packed with detailed time references that allow a full presentation of particulars and that justify the inclusion of non-narrative material. By varying material and altering chronology, Richardson gives the novel interesting and flexible rhythms. Time, moreover, becomes a potent influence on the movement of the plot and on the inner lives of the characters, most significantly as it operates on Clarissa herself. *Clarissa* is an impressive accomplishment, not least because of its intricate tapestry of time.

III. Time in *Sir Charles Grandison*

In its treatment of time, *Sir Charles Grandison* is a curious blend of the merits of *Clarissa* and the defects of *Pamela,* its strongest affinities being, unfortunately, with the latter. It follows a calendar of dates that is systematically worked out, with letters and documents identified with day of composition and often, as in *Clarrisa,* with the hour or moment further specified. The unit of time that encompasses the action of *Grandison* is approximately eighteen months, a period almost twice as long as that recorded in *Clarissa,* but considerably more space is devoted to the events of the first four months of the action than to those of the last fourteen. Letters dated from January 10 to May 17 take up the first two thirds of the novel's total bulk, while over a year is covered by the remaining third. There is, consequently, less of the concentrated, minute-by-minute coverage than is found in *Clarissa,* although there are no significant gaps in the action, Richardson having taken pains to explain hiatuses in the correspondence. A footnote, for example, to a letter dated Monday, July 23, explains that "Several letters, written in the space between the last date, June 16, and the present, which give an account of their diversions, visits, entertainment, at Selby House, Shirley Manor, &c., are omitted" (V, 108). The letters themselves contain time references ("last evening," "this afternoon"), although, in general, they are neither so minutely discriminated nor so frequent as the time references in *Clarissa.* But, while its formal techniques establish a framework of time that should allow as versatile and meaningful a treatment of time as that found in *Clarissa, Grandison* is nevertheless inferior to its predecessor for reasons that become clear as the two are contrasted further.

For the most part, only a tenuous connection is evident in *Sir Charles Grandison* between the actions depicted and the times at which they are presumed to have occurred. That is, although situations develop and time sequences can be identified, the coupling of dates with actions seems to be an essentially arbitrary procedure. This, of course, is in marked contrast to the early establishment in

Clarissa of a context of time relationships out of which later events develop. After the opening letters of *Grandison*, which serve to introduce Harriet Byron, her suitors, and her new social contacts in London, a plot situation of sorts develops in Sir Hargrave Pollexfen's unsuccessful pursuit of Harriet, his abduction of her from a masquerade ball, and her subsequent rescue by Sir Charles. But the sequence conveys nothing of the sense of conflict enlarged through time that pervades the Harlowe-Lovelace-Clarissa antagonisms. Sir Hargrave is introduced as a new acquaintance of Harriet, with nothing suggesting future complications in the relationship, each stage of which then develops almost independently. Sir Hargrave's proposal, for example, occurs at their second meeting; his anger at Harriet's rebuff is presented in a lengthy comic scene, following which Harriet makes this observation:

> Thus did Sir Hargrave confirm all that Sir John Allestree had said of his bad qualities: and I think I am more afraid of him than ever I was of any man before. I remember, that *mischievous* is one of the bad qualities Sir John attributed to him: and *revengeful* another. Should I ever see him again on the same errand, I will be more explicit as to my being absolutely disengaged in my affections, if I can be so without giving him hope, lest he should do private mischief to some one on my account. Upon my word, I would not, of all the men I have ever seen, be the wife of Sir Hargrave Pollexfen (I, 107).

But Harriet's apprehensions about future encounters carry no real conviction and establish little expectancy in the reader, for this encounter has been sandwiched in among other tete-a-tetes in which Harriet has been involved, its import appearing to be no more weighty than a demonstration of Harriet's failure to be impressed by wealth or bombast. The passage does not reverberate with the sense of time found in Clarissa's reaction to her surprise meeting with Lovelace at the Harlowe woodhouse. In consequence of the unsubstantial significance of time, the events and characters of *Grandison* remain far more generalized than those in *Clarissa*. Sir Hargrave, as determined rake, has none of the particularity at a point in time of Lovelace, just as later, Sir Charles will appear as manly virtue in a timeless world. Everything illustrates, but nothing engrosses.

The fully articulated time scheme of *Grandison*, then, serves no real function in particularizing either the narrative or the actors. It likewise has little influence on the non-narrative sections of the

novel. In *Clarissa,* because the time schedule is related meaningfully to the action, the framework of dated correspondence becomes
a serviceable technique for the inclusion of generalized discourse.
In *Grandison,* despite the regular dating of letters, Richardson re-
verts to the procedure of *Pamela II,* in which the reflective, discursive, or analytical passages have no real temporal affinity to the
contexts from which they spring. Thus, instead of the fluid rhythms
and careful pacing of *Clarissa, Grandison* suffers from a monotony
of movement, there being no valid reason why the narrative should
so steadily yield to social definitions and descriptions of manners.
Sir Charles's advice to his sister concerning the duties of a wife, for
example, is simply one of a multitude of reflections on marriage that
are occasioned by Charlotte's impending wedding:

> If, Charlotte, said he, you would have the world around you respect
> your husband, *you* must set the example. While the wife gives the
> least room to suspect that she despises her husband, she will find that
> she subjects him to double contempt, if he resents it not; and if he
> does, can you be happy? Aggressors lay themselves open to severe
> reprisals. If you differ, you will be apt to make by-standers judges
> over you. They will remember, when you are willing to forget; and
> your fame will be the sport of those beneath you, as well in under-
> standing as degree (IV, 181).

This sententious material might occur at any point, before, during,
or after a wedding, or without a wedding taking place. The thread
that stitches it to a developing plot is extremely thin.

A major result of the weaknesses described above is that they
preclude the structural use of time that operates so powerfully in
Clarissa. Here it is obvious that Richardson's total concept of the
nature of the novel shifts back in emphasis to the indoctrinatory intentions of *Pamela,* that is, to the establishment of a narrative vehicle that carries the messages but remains subordinate to them,
both in function and in importance. Time, then, as an operative
force on human intentions and behavior, has little relevance either
to such a vehicle or to its freight. The characters in *Grandison,* consequently, never really confront the pressures of time, nor are they
aware of time as part of the quality of experience. There is always
leisure for debate, for reaching the correct, exemplary decision.
Even such a quandary as Sir Charles's choice between Harriet and
Clementina is resolved to everyone's satisfaction on the basis of an

abstract principle (as a Catholic, Clementina cannot marry Sir Charles), the emotions being as generalized as the theory. The consequent anemic quality that characterizes *Grandison* as a novel results, of course, from more than Richardson's failure to duplicate his handling of time in *Clarissa*. But the contrasts between the two novels clearly demonstrate the importance of time and time relationships in the creation of a successful novel. If, as suggested earlier, time, character, and action are interdependent in achieving both their particularity and their ultimate meanings, a novelist cannot weaken one without weakening the others. The full employment of time in *Clarissa* parallels a full exploration of character and action, with a resulting plenitude of embodied meaning. The arbitrary connections among time, character, and action in *Grandison* parallel a casual dispersement of meaning into a series of artificially regulated and mutually isolated segments of generalized observations.

We turn now to time's correlative, space.

IV. Intervening Space

Specific physical locations can take on individuality as we
become aware of the space that intervenes between one place and
another. From the beginning, novels have presented action within
arrangements of space that are proportioned as in life. A fixed point
(whether implied, named, or described in detail) marks the location
of a given act, but at various distances away from the fixed center
exist other places, persons, and actions (whether or not they are
ever presented). A novel's horizontal distances are revealed in
many ways. Defoe's literalness underscores the distances that are
implied by the motion of his characters, Moll Flanders, for example,
reporting a trip to Bath, "which was about fifteen miles, as I remem-
ber." The goals of Fielding's characters — to get to London, to get
back to the country, to overtake, to elude — likewise establish linear
perspective. Even smaller arenas have their related points; when
a Jane Austen heroine walks to a shop she travels a radius from the
center of a circle to a point on the circumference that in turn becomes the center of a circle. As soon as a reader perceives horizontal
distances in a novel, he sees patterns of space that he knows in his
own experience. Consequently, the reader is sensitive to infinitely
more space than actually becomes a part of the novel's subject matter. He knows that roads lead to other roads, that hills provide
vistas, that here implies there. The spaces between the actual locations of action in novels become as significantly real to the reader
as the locations themselves. Thus, Richardson, in common with
novelists of his own century and of the two centuries following, can
suggest to the reader, without even applying much conscious art-
istry, that one location is related to another in a proportioned spatial
arrangement.

Intervening space is implied, for example, by the epistolary
situations in Richardson's novels. The likelihood, however, of the
reader's becoming conscious of the distance between the point
where a letter is composed and the point where it is received depends, as does the reader's willingness to assign significance to that
distance, on the relevance of the distance to the letter. If Harriet
Byron discusses the assembled company at a dinner party, giving a

"description of their persons and characters" (I, xlvii); if Pamela evaluates a play she has seen in London and "censures severely the epilogue" (IV, vi); if Clarissa sets forth her views on pride and humility, their letters do not suggest the relative locations of writer and recipient, nor do they need to. If, on the other hand, Pamela tells her father and mother about the home-spun gown that she is preparing for her return to them, her letter urges into the reader's consciousness a sense of the distance between Pamela and her parents. Likewise, if Lovelace directs Belford to hasten to Clarissa's rescue, his letter strongly illustrates that Belford is one place and Lovelace another. By and large, however, epistolary distance is a relatively unimportant type of space in Richardson's novels, for the central characters seldom correspond directly with one another. The recipients, therefore, tend to be just that, with little significance attaching to their locations.[7]

The sense of intervening space that the reader receives from Richardson's novels is stimulated in a second way, not necessarily related to the epistolary machinery. The movement of the action from one location to another tends to formulate plot and geography into parallel patterns, made up, in both cases, of fixed points connected by imaginary lines. In the case of plot patterns, the lines consist of the causal elements that account for the arrival at a given point in the action or suggest further development to another point. In the case of geographic patterns, the lines consist of the intervening space that has been or is likely to be traversed. *Clarissa* provides the best example here, although the other two novels illustrate the principle also. Both patterns begin at Harlowe Place, where the various embroilments suggest a furtherance of the plot situation and a removal to another location. Lovelace takes Clarissa to St. Albans, and again both situational and geographic problems must be solved, with the alternatives in both cases finally narrowing down to London, and more specifically to the lodgings at Mrs. Sinclair's.

---

[7] Some of the awkwardness of the epistolary technique results, in fact, from the very necessity of establishing space between writer and recipient. Thus Belford constantly seems to be hastening out of town to a deathbed so that Lovelace can write rather than speak to him. Lucy Selby is kept out of the thick of things so that Harriet can describe them for her. And to a lesser extent, Anna Howe is also stage-managed on and off at appropriate times.

Tensions develop here and Clarissa escapes to Hampstead, fleeing both a condition and a place. Lovelace retrieves her, and back at the Sinclair lodgings, effects the rape, a place and an action that demand further flight. Clarissa escapes to Covent Garden, is arrested and confined at an officer's house, but is finally returned to the room from which she is to make her final escape to death. Thus, at a half a dozen points the spatial and causal lines converge and strike out in new directions, promoting the unifying significance of the distances that extend as the novel proceeds. It is worth observing here, that two of the primary settings, Harlowe Place and the Sinclair lodgings, are the most difficult places to leave behind; the departures must be effected in stages. Thus they are not only spatially and causally significant, but are also focused thematically, and the physical interval between them, as sensed by the reader, is of major importance. In *Pamela I*, a similar, although less complex, pattern of parallels can be noted in the shift from Bedfordshire to Lincolnshire, and in *Grandison*, a sense of movement pervades the narration of Sir Charles's Italian adventures, but *Pamela II* and other sections of *Grandison* display a static quality that discourages a perception of proportioned space.

A third process that suggests intervening space to the reader is the development within the spokesmen themselves of an awareness of distances. Such awareness is generally the accompaniment of a critical turn in the development of the plot, and is, in fact, an outgrowth of the parallel patterns of geography and action examined above. When, for example, Pamela has started what she regards as the journey home, her thoughts vacillate between her place of departure and her destination:

> Well, said I to myself, at this rate I shall soon be with my dear father and mother; and till I had got, as I supposed, halfway, I thought of the good friends I had left: And when, on stopping for a little bait to the horses, Robin told me I was nearly half way, I thought it was high time to wipe my eyes, and think to whom I was going . . . So I began to ponder what a meeting I should have with you; how glad you'd both be to see me come safe and innocent to you, after all my dangers: and so I began to comfort myself, and to banish the other gloomy side from my mind; though, too, it returned now and then; for I should be ungrateful not to love them for their love (I, 105).

When she begins to suspect something amiss, she is still concerned
with spatial relationships: "Hey-day, thought I, to drive this strange
pace, and to be so long a going a little more than twenty miles, is
very odd!" (*Ibid.*). And when, upon the entrance of Mrs. Jewkes,
the full impact of the stratagem strikes her, she is completely frus-
trated by the directional reverse: "I was forced to set out with
[Mrs. Jewkes] in the chariot . . . and now I gave over all thoughts of
redemption, and was in a desponding condition indeed" (I, 111).
Although the reader may fail to share Pamela's reactions, he is not
likely to miss the triangular pattern of space that her dilemma suggests, as the points marked by Bedfordshire and home connect with
the new destination in Lincolnshire. In a different situation, Harriet
Byron also becomes painfully aware of the personal force of space.
When Sir Charles abruptly leaves for Italy, Harriet describes their
final evening:

> When we broke up, he handed my cousin Reeves into her coach.
> He handed me. Mr. Reeves said, We see you again Sir Charles, in
> the morning? He bowed. At handing me in, he sighed — he pressed
> my hand — I think he did — that was all — he saluted nobody. He
> will not meet his Clementina as he parted with us (IV, 229).

The last sentence of the passage suddenly gives extended linear
perspective to an otherwise localized account. Harriet, her own
emotions now admittedly involved, can visualize Sir Charles with
her rival, as can the reader.[8] Harriet's consciousness of his absence
continues to rattle her until the spatial gap is closed. For Lovelace,
the sense of separation from Clarissa is intensified almost to a condition of physical torture. It begins while she is confined at Harlowe
Place, is strengthened with each of her escapes, and reaches its great-
est power when she lies dying:

> Forbidden to attend the dear creature, yet longing to see her. I
> would give the world to be admitted once more to her beloved pres-
> ence. I ride towards London three or four times a day, resolving *pro*
> and *con*, twenty times in two or three miles; and at last ride back;
> and, in view of Uxbridge, loathing even the kind friend and hos-
> pitable house, turn my horse's head again towards the town (VIII,
> 42).

---

[8] Such a stroke as this reveals more about Harriet's attitude than do paragraphs
of her expressed admiration for Clementina. One wishes Richardson had
left it at this.

Lovelace's mental turmoil is here closely associated with the space that bars him from his object; every mile is a palpable enemy. Passages such as the ones quoted above combine so many elements in addition to spatial considerations — elements of plot, character, motive, and theme — that it is difficult to single out a dominant intention or a dominant result. But they all clearly give us characters at moments when space has intervened and when an awareness of that intervention has influenced both the process of thought and the process of communication. Of the three conditions we have examined in which Richardson's novels transmit to the reader a sense of action conducted within arrangements of space that are proportioned as in life, this third, the depiction of such a consciousness in the spokesmen, is the most viable.

V. Confined Space

Intervening space is but one aspect of the total physical environment that a novelist attempts to supply. Another aspect, and in Richardson perhaps a more important one, is confined space, the unit that does not simply extend horizontally between locations but that is a location itself, captured in all dimensions and deriving its significance both from within and from without. In Richardson, confined space develops partly from the repeated theme of imprisonment that typifies his work. Certainly, in *Pamela* and *Clarissa* a large share of the action takes place within the walls of the heroines' prisons; and even in *Grandison* the theme recurs in the abduction of Harriet by Pollexfen and in the confinement of Clementina by her family. But we are here concerned not so much with space as prison as we are with space as entity and with the means by which such space is created or suggested.

The fully realized setting, its attributes by themselves (and not as associated with the other aspects of a novel) producing in the reader a sensory response, is found infrequently in Richardson's novels, and, indeed, is rare in the works of most of the early novelists. Recent critics, attempting to educe a theory of realism from the 18th-century novel, have noted this absence. Dorothy Van Ghent, for example, in dealing with Defoe's realism, argues that

> In saying . . . the world of *Moll Flanders* is made up to a large extent of *things,* we do not mean that it is a world rich in physical, sensuous textures — in images for the eye or for the tactile sense or for the tongue or the ear or for the sense of temperature or the sense of pressure. It is extraordinarily barren of such images.[9]

Ian Watt, also in search of a defining principle of realism, notes that Fielding "gives us no full interiors and his frequent landscape descriptions are very conventionalized."[10] With Smollett, the novel begins to particularize sensory reaction — most vividly, in Smollett, reaction to the unpleasant stimuli of stench and filth — for, as Walter

---

[9] *The English Novel: Form and Function* (New York, 1953), p. 35.
[10] *The Rise of the Novel* (Berkeley, 1957), p. 27.

Allen suggests, Smollett is a man "affronted in all his senses by life as he has experienced it." [11] But not until later in its history — with the coming of the Gothic romance, the historical novel, and the novel of manners — do we find the novel consistently employing confined and particularized space to create a response of physical presence. While we do not find such a treatment of space as a consistent process in Richardson, we do find it occasionally, as we will note, and we find other means and other reasons for placing the action in a comprehensible setting. As in so many other matters, Richardson operates as if he had at his disposal the whole range of aims and techniques that have come to typify the novel since he wrote his three. In this matter, we find little reason to suspect that he selected the wrong ones.

Not surprisingly, the epistolary mode provides Richardson with one method for suggesting confined space. We must first observe that if Richardson does not describe a setting in full sensory detail, he does not thereby prevent his reader from understanding its characteristics. Just as the reader will apply his own experience of spatial relationships to those suggested in a novel, he will also apply his understanding of actual locations to their fictional counterparts. Richardson could expect, therefore, that the readers of his society would grasp the various confines of space in his novels on the basis of their knowledge of their own surroundings; it doesn't require too active an effort of historical imagination for readers of later societies to interpret his signals. Richardson is, furthermore, operating within a relatively young tradition, one that takes as a distinguishing characteristic the names of objects, places, and persons as if from life. The novel's documentary realism, creating an "illusion of verifiable fact," [12] often stops short with the name and does not continue to supply physical attributes, but the accumulation of names — familiar in themselves to the reader — can suggest associated traits. Richardson's entire plan is, in effect, a form of documentary realism, since the epistolary collection is presumed to recreate an activity recognized in life. Hence, the writing of letters — "naming" them as verifiable documents — suggests places wherein they are composed. Further, the objects associated with their composition — the pens, ink, paper, desks, chairs, locked doors, hiding places —; the

---

[11] *The English Novel* (London, 1954), p. 65.
[12] The phrase is Van Ghent's (p. 33), used by her with reference to Defoe.

physical conditions that influence the writer — lighting, privacy, health —; and the activities included in the writing — alluding, quoting, cross-referencing, enclosing — all convey aspects of imaginable environments to the reader. Just as it suggests intervening space, the epistolary format, then, also postulates confined space, space that in reading Richardson we become aware of and attach significance to as it assumes relevance to the subject matter of the letters. Our impression of Anna Howe's surroundings as she writes, for example, is far more vague than our sense of Clarissa's. But it is neverthless there as part of our apprehension of Anna, even though scarcely a word exists in direct description of the Howe residence.

We find often that Richardson's details, in their factual realism, carry implications of confined space. Like Defoe, in fact, he will enumerate objects with an eye to the standard of living, and hence to the environment, they represent:

> Since my last [writes Pamela in an early letter], my master gave me more fine things. He called me up to my late lady's closet, and, pulling out her drawers, he gave me two suits of fine Flanders laced head-clothes, three pair of fine silk shoes, two hardly the worse . . . and the other with wrought silver buckles in them; and several ribands and top-knots of all colours; four pair of white fine cotton stockings, and three pair of fine silk ones; and two pair of rich stays. I was quite astonished and unable to speak for a while . . . (I, 10).

This finery, in the absence of explicit portrayal of the B. estate, effectively allows the reader to visualize Pamela's surroundings. Similarly, in the preamble (itself a "verifiable" document) to the controversial will of Clarissa's grandfather, the details suggest a degree of opulence in the surroundings far beyond anything directly presented in description of Harlowe Place:

> . . . as my three sons have been uncommonly prosperous, and are very rich: the eldest by means of the unexpected benefits he reaps from his new found mines; the second, by what has, as unexpectedly, fallen in to him on the deaths of several relations of his present wife . . . over and above the very large portion which he received with her in marriage; my son Antony by his East India traffic, and successful voyages: as furthermore my grandson James will be sufficiently provided for by his grandmother Lovell's kindness to him; who, having no near relations, hath assured me, that she hath, as well by deed of gift as

by will, left him both her Scottish and English estates: for never was
there a family more prosperous in all its branches, blessed be God
therefore . . . (I, 26).

Here, as elsewhere, Richardson supplies an appropriate set of details
to trigger the reader's factual understanding of the setting, even
though the details do not stimulate a sensory response. We are
given the basis for an appraisal and we are free to envision the
entity appraised. In like manner, the details of action may serve to
portray space for the reader, especially if the action, in its violence
or its emotion, brings the characters into direct physical contact
with the tangibles of their environment. The fire scene in *Clarissa*
is a colorful example as Lovelace presents it to Belford:

> Mrs. Sinclair's cookmaid . . . , having sat up to read the simple *His-
> tory of Dorastus and Faunia,* when she should have been in bed, had
> set fire to an old pair of calico window-curtains.
>
>   She had the presence of mind, in her fright, to tear down the
> half-burnt vallens, as well as curtains, and had got them, though blaz-
> ing, into the chimney by the time I came up . . . (V, 14).

The account that follows — of Lovelace rushing to Clarissa's door,
lifting her into bed, debating with her, retreating, and returning to
plead — is a brilliant realization of the *mise-en-scene* by means of
action. The reader is made thoroughly aware of the physical peri-
meters of the action and of the substantial fixtures that exist within.[13]

The reader, then, is able to learn by an inferential process a
great deal about the encompassing space in Richardson's novels,
more, in fact, than he learns from the generalized statements that
frequently introduce a change of scenery for the action. That is, if,
as in the passages cited above, details are presented that name contents, or causes, or equipment, or activities in specific terms, the
environmental picture created in the reader's mind is more vivid
than it would be if only qualities or attributes were named. For
example, this statement, "My cousins' house is suitable to their
fortune: very handsome and furnished in taste" (*Grandison,* I, 14),
while no more concrete in its descriptive endeavor than the preamble to the will, conveys a less substantial image of confined space.
So it is that many locations are never rescued from their generalized

---

[13] A scene that similarly employs the details of action to suggest the surrounding space, is Pamela's attempted escape from her Lincolnshire prison.

limbo: "a stately, well-furnished, and convenient house," "my apart-
ment is extremely elegant," "a handsome parlour, elegantly furnished." [14] In such statements, Richardson counts on the reader to
imagine the setting, but gives him little help. Occasionally, the
reader encounters a passage that reveals an almost Imlacian neglect
of the "minuter discriminations," a good example being the following treatment of Sir Charles's alterations at Grandison Hall:

> He has a great taste . . . yet not an expensive one; for he studies situ-
> ation and convenience, and pretends not to level hills, or to force
> and distort nature; but to help it, as he finds it, without letting art be
> seen in his works, where he can possibly avoid it. For he says, he
> would rather let a stranger be pleased with what he sees, as if it
> were always so; than to obtain comparative praise by informing
> him what it was in its former situation (III, 244).

But such generalized matter usually is appropriate to the intention
of the narrative where it appears. That is, the reader feels no need
for a more specific treatment of space; for, as we shall now observe,
if specific description is useful, it is supplied.

The primary characteristic of the passages in Richardson that
appear to be straight descriptions of setting is that they nearly
always illustrate the reporter's state of mind. The significance of
this will perhaps be clearer if we recall that to this point we have
observed processes whereby confined space is suggested or implied,
rather than specified. The theme of imprisonment, the epistolary
mode, the authoritative details, and the generalized statements all
allow the reader to regard the action as being conducted within spatial units that are, if not familiar, at least imaginable. But with the
possible exception of the generalized statements about places, the
primary intent of the elements we have examined has been something other than the establishment of setting. In other words, the
spatial units inferred by the reader are the byproducts of techniques
employed to serve other ends. When we encounter, then, a process
that would appear to have as its primary purpose the depiction of
setting but that also performs the important function of presenting
a character's mental state, we have reason to suspect that here also,
the spatial concern might be secondary. And when, as we shall also

---

[14] The quotations are, in order, from *Pamela*, III, 309; *Grandison*, I, 14; and
Grandison, I, 168.

observe, the placement of passages that contain minute environmental details is often at odds with what might be their ordinary
novelistic function, we have further reason to conclude that the
Richardsonian procedure does not take as a major aim the direct
creation of a physical setting. Nevertheless, a workable physical
setting does emerge from the Richardsonian procedure, and not
only emerges but becomes an impressive aspect of the author's
accomplishment.

Illustration of the point can begin with *Pamela.* I have observed
that for its first hundred pages *Pamela* presents what amounts to a
hypothetical case in a timeless world and that after Pamela's arrival
at the Lincolnshire estate, the introduction of a well-documented
time scheme gives particularity to the action. I have also noted
that Mr. B.'s Bedfordshire estate (Pamela's residence during the
first hundred pages) is rendered as a place primarily by circum-
stantial details rather than by direct description. Pamela here re-
ports her arrival at its counterpart, the Lincolnshire estate:

> About eight at night, we entered the courtyard of this handsome,
> large, old, and lonely mansion, that looks made for solitude and mis-
> chief, as I thought, by its appearance, with all its brown nodding hor-
> rors of lofty elms and pines about it: and here, said I to myself, I
> fear, is to be the scene of my ruin, unless God protect me, who is
> all-sufficient! (I, 112-113).

While rather general in its terms (the elms and the pines are about
the only specific details), the passage nevertheless provides a much
more explicit exterior view of the mansion than anything we are
told about the Bedfordshire place; hence it aids the particularization
of action that begins in this section. But the details are clearly
selected to show the effect of the place on Pamela's mind, the threat
to her virtue for the first time being embodied in the physical world
that surrounds her. A happier mood is reflected in the following
passage from *Pamela II*. Mrs. B. is describing her husband's proposed renovations at the Kentish farm where he has established the
elderly Andrews couple:

> The old bay windows he will have preserved, but will not have
> them sashed, nor the woodbines, jessamines, and vines that have run
> up against them, destroyed; only he will have larger panes of glass,
> and convenienter casements, to let in more of the sweet air and light,
> to make amends for that obstructed by the shades of those fragrant
> climbers . . .

> The parlour indeed will be more elegant; though that is to be rather plain than rich, as well in its wainscot as furniture, and to be new floored. The dear gentleman has already given orders about it, and you will soon have workmen with you to put them in execution. The parlour doors are to have brass hinges and locks, and to shut as close, he tells them, as a watch-case . . . (II, 286).

These alterations are mentioned once again; when Pamela and her husband visit the Kentish farm, B. is pleased with the results (IV, 145). Otherwise, the details have no significance except to illustrate Pamela's delight at B.'s generosity toward her parents — no important action is conducted in the setting that in any way depends on the reader's knowledge of the "convenienter casements" or the brass hinges. This, then, is space confined by the reaction it produces in the spokesman.

Clarissa supplies additional examples of particularized space that reveals mental qualities. Chafing under the strictures of her family, Clarissa is forced to arrange a clandestine correspondence with Anna Howe. She describes a proposed point of exchange for their letters in these terms:

> You must remember the Green Lane, as we call it, that runs by the side of the wood-house and poultry-yard where I keep my bantams, pheasants, and pea-hens, which generally engage my notice twice a day; the more my favourites because they were my grandfather's, and recommended to my care by him; and therefore brought hither from my dairy-house since his death.
>
> The lane is lower than the floor of the wood-house; and in the side of the wood-house the boards are rotted away down to the floor for half an ell together in several places. Hannah can step into the lane and make a mark with a chalk where a letter or parcel may be pushed in, under some sticks; which may be so managed as to be an unsuspected cover for the written deposits from either (I, 47).

Although the details here work effectively to create for the reader a strong sense of place — the rotting boards and the chalk are particularly successful stimuli to sensory response — Richardson builds the passage with his heroine's qualities uppermost in his intentions. The hiding place itself could be established without reference to Clarissa's applied poultry husbandry or to her sentiments toward her grandfather; and in the description of the woodhouse, Clarissa's ingenuity — not to mention her determination — is a dominant element. The hiding place simply adds a dramatic embellishment to

the machinery of the correspondence and to the plight — not yet
overly serious — of the heroine. When Clarissa's plight later does
become serious, we encounter perhaps the most extensive and detailed description of setting in the novel in Belford's report to Lovelace of his visit to the officer's house where Clarissa is confined following her second escape from Mrs. Sinclair's. Richardson is here
interested in dramatizing the emotions of Belford, who has now
almost completely shifted his allegiance from Lovelace to Clarissa.
As he describes the house, therefore, Belford piles horror on horror
in a crescendo that builds to his ringing contrast between Clarissa
and her surroundings:

> A horrid hole of a house, in an alley they call a court; stairs
> wretchedly narrow, even to the first-floor room: and into a den they
> led me, with broken walls, which had been papered, as I saw by a
> multitude of tacks, and some torn bits held on by the rusty heads.
>
> The floor indeed was clean, but the ceiling was smoked with a
> variety of figures, and initials of names, that had been the woful em-
> ployment of wretches who had no other way to amuse themselves. . .
>
> The windows dark and double-barred; the tops boarded up to
> save mending; and only a little four-paned eyelet-hole of a casement
> to let in air; more however, coming in at broken panes than could
> come in at that. . . .
>
> To finish the shocking description, in a dark nook stood an old
> broken-bottomed cane couch, without a squab, or coverlid, sunk at
> one corner, and unmortised by the failing of one of its worm-eaten
> legs, which lay in two pieces under the wretched piece of furniture
> it could no longer support.
>
> And this, thou horrid Lovelace, was the bed-chamber of the
> divine Clarissa! ! ! (VI, 258-259).

The elaborateness of this account[15] is pointless as preparation for
action to be conducted within the setting, for Clarissa is soon returned to her lodgings at the Smiths'. But the passage functions
effectively to secure Belford's perception of the injury Clarissa has
suffered at the hands of Lovelace. Richardson's main aim, conse-

---

[15] I have quoted slightly less than half of the entire descriptive passage, the
sections not quoted containing details of a similar nature. A few pages
later, Belford presents Clarissa's lodgings at the Smiths' in general terms:
"She has two handsome apartments, a bed-chamber and dining-room,
with light closets in each" (VI, 276). The lack of particularization in
this setting has implications of its own, as we will shortly observe.

quently, is to account for the highly wrought state of Belford; the vivid unit of space that he creates is a means to that end.

In *Grandison*, we encounter a curious section in which descriptive material is so placed that it cannot provide a backdrop for action, as one would ordinarily expect it to do, but is so prominent that it cannot be ignored as inconsequential. Throughout the novel numerous locations are presented with varying degrees of particularity,[16] but not until the final volume, when everything is over but the mopping up, does Grandison Hall receive descriptive attention, and then with such regard for minutia as to make it the most reproduceable setting in all Richardson (VIII, 40-52). We are given everything but the blueprint ("It is built in the form of an H") and we are introduced systematically to the house and its contents, the park, gardens and orchard around it, the parish church, and the picture gallery. The production of an elaborate descriptive passage at this point appears to be gratuitous, unless the passage is taken as a testimony to the good fortune of Harriet (and the good taste of Sir Charles), and there is a strong possibility that this is Richardson's intention. The letters that contain the description are written by Harriet and begin with an exclamation that specifically equates Grandison Hall with Harriet's pleasure: "Oh my dearest, dearest grandmamma! Here I am! The declared mistress of this spacious house, and the happiest of human creatures!" (VII, 39). What better way to illustrate the degree of Harriet's rapture than by diagramming the cause? Moreover, in presenting the description, Harriet is taking over a function already contracted for by Lucy Selby,[17] and the rationalization for her doing so is flimsy at best:

> Lucy says she will be very particular in her letters. This will take up time; especially as Lady G - - - - and Lady L - - - - must see them in their way to Northamptonshire; although they will not detain

---

[16] See, for example, Mr. Reeve's account to George Selbey of the tracking down of Harriet (I, 159). Richardson's characters appear to be most observant of their surroundings when they are on the march. Also see Mr. Lowther's report of his trip with Sir Charles across the mountains to Parma (V, 17-20). Such a forceful presentation of the natural world (with snow, ice, and rough terrain) seems as foreign to the normal world of Richardson as would the sudden appearance of an astronaut.

[17] The description of the grounds and surrounding terrain is, in fact, written by Lucy and included as a footnote to Harriet's letter (VII, 44-45).

them. I shall have an opportunity to send this to London on Monday.
This makes me intend to snatch every opportunity of writing. It will
otherwise be too long before you will hear of us by my hand.

I do not intend to invade this slow girl's province; yet I will give
you a slight sketch of the house and apartments, as I go along (VII,
42-43).

Richardson apparently decided that the ecstasies of his heroine
could best be presented by allowing her, rather than Lucy, to describe her new toy.

In each of the three novels, then, we find that the more particularized treatments of confined space appear in substantiation of
the reporters' mental processes. It seems legitimate to suggest, on
the basis of this observation, that Richardson acutely perceives an
interaction between environment and psychology and that he sees
the reality of spatial units in the flux between the general and the
particular, each unit becoming meaningful and specific itself as it
influences a specific mind. If Richardson is regarded as a transi-
tional figure between two traditions — one that regards experience
as universal, the common activity of mankind, and one that regards
experience as particular, the unique response of an individual to the
phenomena of life — no more significant evidence could be cited
than his treatment of confined space. For in noting that space is
both an assumption — imbedded in themes, techniques, details, and
general statements — and also an operative stimulus to the mental
life of the characters, we see the neo-classical mind meeting the
modern mind; Imlac linking arms with Dickens, James, and Kafka;
the prose narrative becoming the novel. And this leads us to the
final type of space that we encounter in Richardson's work, transmuted space.

VI. Transmuted Space

In a preceding section, we observed a fusion of time and action that gives a structure of dramatic inevitability to *Clarissa* unlike anything found in either *Pamela* or *Grandison*. We likewise find in *Clarissa* a quality of space that is unique among Richardson's novels, a powerful quality that supercharges the physical locations of the novel until they crackle with energy. This quality I term transmuted space, for it results when the material properties of an environment merge to become a moral force in the non-material precincts that are the ultimate setting for the novel's action. Dorothy Van Ghent speaks of the tendency in *Clarissa* "to convert the external forms of life . . . into subjective quality and spiritual value." (p. 45), a tendency that she traces in Richardson's myth-making treatment of characters in a context of religious and social values and that we have observed in his equation of spatial units with the emotion of the witness. When the delimiting space of the physical world yields to the infinitude of the moral realm, space is transmuted from entity to essence. I shall now examine this transmutation as it occurs in three of the major locations in *Clarissa*.

We begin with Harlowe Place. Nowhere is this familial estate accorded a physical description with the plentiude of detail that we encounter in Harriet's presentation of Grandison Hall, yet it becomes, in the words of Ian Watt, "a terrifyingly real physical and moral environment." (p. 27). How is this accomplished? We have already observed one method whereby the material qualities are suggested, the employment of details weighted with implications from which the reader can derive a factual understanding of the setting. Thus, the preamble to the will of Clarissa's grandfather posits an opulence of architecture and furnishings that is not delineated to any extent. The moral qualities of Harlowe Place likewise develop through the accumulation of details, but details of another order. An expanding portrayal of attitudes, convictions, and motives infuses the estate with conflicting qualities and the resultant tension animates in the reader a moral judgment. The internal discord of the Harlowe family, initiated by the grandfather's will and complicated by the involvements with Lovelace, first establishes the aura of greed that emanates from the Harlowe holdings. On the inside, Clarissa early isolates the moral issue involved in the pressure on her to accept the favor of Solmes:

> One great estate is already obtained at the expense of the relations to it, though distant relations; my brother's I mean, by his godmother: and this has given the hope, however chimerical that hope, of procuring others; and that my own at least may revert to the family. And yet, in my opinion, the world is but one great family. Originally it was so. What then is this narrow selfishness that reigns in us, but relationship remembered against relationship forgot? (I, 41).

Here the explicit contrast between "one great estate" and "one great family," [18] with its overtones of material versus spiritual values, blights the expansive acreage with the moral atrophy of the Harlowes. From the outside, Anna Howe is initially the observer who descries the taint:

> Your grandfather knew the family-failing. He knew what a noble spirit you had to do good. He himself perhaps . . . had done too little in his lifetime; and therefore he put it in your power to make up for the defects of the whole family. Were it to me, I would resume it. Indeed I would (I, 152).

The corrupt drives of the Harlowes as embodied in their property are later epitomized in a brief simile by their major antagonist, Lovelace: "Everybody knows Harlowe Place, for, like Versailles, it is sprung up from a dunghill" (I, 208). Thus, before the real problems of the Lovelace-Clarissa struggle are under way, Harlowe Place is transformed from a physical location to a moral environment.

But the Harlowe mansion is not left simply as a symbol of the forces of greed that operate within it. It comes to embody a universal judgment on any corruptive force that deprives an individual of his integrity, hence sins against life itself.[19] After the action of the novel shifts to London, Harlowe Place continues to loom in the background as the implacable force that has compelled Clarissa's flight and that blocks her return, both literally, in the position as-

---

[18] One might find this contrast ironic, but Clarissa and Richardson here probably use "family" as a concept of the Harlowes as they should be, not as they are.

[19] ". . . had they trusted to a discretion which they owned she had never brought into question, she would have extricated them and herself . . . from all difficulties as to Lovelace" (VIII, 321-322).

sumed by its inhabitants, and morally, in its establishment of an impenetrable evil that cannot harbor the good it has rejected. During her final weeks, Clarissa writes letter after letter to the members of her family and is repulsed by each. Her sister finally makes a proposal that announces the moral death of the Harlowes in their supreme concern with material over spiritual values:

> I have another proposal to make to you, and that in the name of every one in the family; which is, that you will think of going to Pennsylvania to reside there for some few years till all is blown over: and if it please God to spare you, and your unhappy parents, till they can be satisfied that you behave like a true and uniform penitent; at least till you are one-and-twenty; you may then come back to your own estate, or have the produce of it sent you there, as you shall choose (VII, 264).

And Harlowe Place at last becomes a moral hell, its physical reminders of the dead Clarissa becoming corrosive in their retributive force. While the dispensing of appropriate misery to each member of the Harlowe clan may seem, on the literal level, too pat as a conclusion, the transmutation of Harlowe Place into punitive energy is convincingly appalling in its presentation of shades who walk about the hallways but "shun each other (at the times they were accustomed to meet together), that they might avoid the mutual reproaches of eyes that spoke, when tongues were silent" (VIII, 323).

A more blatant form of evil infuses the Sinclair lodgings, the second location we will consider with regard to transmuted space. The reader is never in doubt about Lovelace's duplicity as he establishes Clarissa in the unsavory household; his explanation to Belford of his tactics for forcing the choice on her while seeming to allow her an unencumbered decision plays in counterpoint to her own uninstructed presentation to Anna. Thus, even before Clarissa is ushered into it, the house takes on sinister connotations. The technique works well here, for had Richardson attempted to lead the reader as unsuspectingly into the trap as he does Clarissa, he would have done so at the expense of the subtlety that arises from allowing the reader to observe the slow dawning of horror in Clarissa herself. Initially, the tone of banter adopted by Lovelace serves to point up the elementary irony in the entrance of a creature of spotless virtue into a rather conventional brothel. It is something of a defiant joke:

> And, among the rest, who dost thou think is to be her maid
> servant? — Deb. Butler.
>
> Ah, Lovelace!
>
> And Ah, Belford! — It can't be otherwise. But what dost think
> Deb's name is to be. Why, Dorcas, Dorcas Wykes. And won't it be
> admirable, if, either through fear, fright, or good liking, we can get
> my beloved to accept of Dorcas Wykes for a bedfellow? (III, 268).

Clarissa's ingenuousness is troubled only slightly by misgivings
about the women of the house (Dorcas has "a strange sly eye. I
never saw such an eye: half-confident, I think. But indeed Mrs. Sinclair herself . . . has an odd winking eye" [III, 273]); but she tries
to withhold judgment in the absence of any positive evidence that
all is not well in the lodgings ("Being very much pressed, I could
not tell how to refuse dining with the widow and her nieces this day.
I am better pleased with them than I ever thought I should be"
[III, 311]). And so, for the time being, the Sinclair house becomes
simply the background for debate between Lovelace and Clarissa,
for various stratagems on both sides to resolve the situation. But
in the continued innocence of Clarissa concerning the nature of her
malodorous surroundings, the reader senses an intensification of the
irony and an ominous quality issuing from the "two good houses,
distant from each other, only joined by a large handsome passage,"
where "the inner house is the genteellest, and very elegantly furnished; but you may have the use of a very handsome parlour in the
outer house, if you choose to look into the street" (III, 170; italics
omitted).

To Clarissa the place becomes intolerable after the fire scene
dramatizes Lovelace's treachery. She escapes to Hampstead and is
tricked back in the company of the women who impersonate Lovelace's relatives:

> Though not pleased, I was nevertheless just then thoughtless of
> danger; they endeavouring thus to lift me up above all apprehension
> of that, and above myself too.
>
> But then, my dear, what a dreadful turn all had upon me, when,
> through several streets and ways I knew nothing of, the coach slack-
> ening its pace, came within sight of the dreadful house of the dread-
> fullest woman in the world; as she proved to me (VI, 160).

So strong is her aversion that it produces a physical reaction:

> My heart misgave me beyond the power of my own accounting
> for it; for still I did not suspect these women. But the antipathy I
> had taken to the vile house, and to find myself so near it, when
> I expected no such matter, with the sight of the old creature, all
> together made me behave like a distracted person (VI, 162).

In this state she is drugged and violated. Now the menacing quality
of the house becomes reality and closes around her in all its carnal-
ity. Clarissa's account of the rape is filled with physical and moral
terror:

> I was so senseless, that I dare not aver, that the horrid creatures
> of the house were personally aiding and abetting: but some visionary
> remembrances I have of female figures, flitting, as I may say, before
> my sight: the wretched woman's particularly. But as these confused
> ideas might be owing to the terror I had conceived of the worse than
> masculine violence she had been permitted to assume to me, for ex-
> pressing my abhorrence to her house; and as what I suffered from his
> barbarity wants not that aggravation; I will say no more on a subject
> as shocking as this must ever be to my remembrance (VI, 169).

In fleeing a second time from the Sinclair house, Clarissa begins her
escape from the world as she now perceives it, a suffusion of mascu-
line, sexual evil of which she must be cleansed. Even the physical
horrors, described in detail by Belford, of her prison in the officer's
house are preferable to the moral horrors she has fled. But we speak
now of Clarissa's reactions. For the reader, the real impact of the
Sinclair lodging comes much later, after Clarissa's death. In the last
volume, during the process of bringing matters to a halt, appears a
long letter from Belford to Lovelace describing the deathbed agonies
of Mrs. Sinclair. Richardson has explicit reasons for including such a
detailed scene at this point; in the synoptical table of contents, he
explains:

> As the bad house is often mentioned in this work without any other
> stigma than what arises from the wretched principles and actions
> occasionally given of the wretches who inhabit it; Mr. Belford here
> enters into the secret retirements of those creatures, and exposes them
> in the appearances they are supposed to make, before they are tricked
> out to ensnare weak and inconsiderate minds (VIII, xii).

Belford himself is given a motive in his desire to clinch Lovelace's
reform by underlining the contrast between a pure woman and a
prostitute:

> What woman, nice in her person, and of purity in her mind and
> manners, did she know what miry wallowers the generality of men
> of our class are in themselves, and constantly trough and sty with, but
> would detest the thoughts of associating with such filthy sensualists,
> whose favourite taste carries them to mingle with the dregs of stews,
> brothels, and common sewers? (VIII, 153).

But the conventional moralizing and warning are of secondary importance for the reader. The scene serves as the final transmutation
of the Sinclair house from the physical to the conceptual level. And
it does so with the most lavish use of sensory, physical details to be
found in the whole novel. When Belford arrives, the old woman,
in the final agonies of a mortified leg, is "raving, crying, cursing, and
even howling, more like a wolf than a human creature" (VIII, 143).
His description of her is a *tour de force* in which the physical details
suggest the gangrenous moral life of the woman:

> Behold her, then, spreading the whole troubled bed with her huge
> quaggy carcass: her mill-post arms held up; her broad hands clenched
> with violence; her big eyes, goggling and flaming red . . . her matted
> grisly hair, made irreverent by her wickedness (her clouted head-
> dress being half off, spread about her fat ears and brawny neck);
> her livid lips parched, and working violently; her broad chin in con-
> vulsive motion; her wide mouth, by reason of the contraction of her
> forehead (which seemed to be half lost in its own frightful furrows)
> splitting her face, as it were, into two parts; and her huge tongue
> hideously rolling in it; heaving, puffing as if for breath; her bellows-
> shaped and various coloured breasts ascending by turns to her chin,
> and descending out of sight, with the violence of her gaspings (VIII,
> 145).

The prostitutes who hover about are presented with equal attention
to detail: "unpropt by stays, squalid, loose in attire, sluggish-haired
. . . eyes half-opened, winking and pinking, mispatched, yawning,
stretching, as if from the unworn-off effects of the midnight revel"
(*Ibid.*). The woman speaks of Clarissa:

> And *is* she dead? — Indeed dead? . . . Oh, what an angel have I been
> the means of destroying! For though it was that wicked man's fault
> that ever she was in my house, yet it was mine, and yours, and yours,
> and yours, devils as we all were . . . that he did not do her justice!
> And that, *that* is my curse, and will one day be yours! And then
> again she howled (VIII, 147).

Although the scene is unduly protracted and suffers from some mis-
placed satire on physicians, it has a cumulative moral intensity that

cannot be ignored. Positioned here at the end of the novel, it re-shapes the previous scenes in the Sinclair environment. What was once an atmosphere of sexual indulgence becomes the realm of personal, aggressive depravity. What was once a standard bawdy house is retroactively transmuted into an ambience of sheer evil.

The last location we will consider with regard to transmuted space is Clarissa's final earthly habitation, the rooms at the Smiths' where, ministered to by Mrs. Lovick and Belford, she acts out the conclusion of her story, for the first time in full control of her own destiny. Clarissa describes her situation to Anna:

> I am no prisoner now in a vile house. I am not now in the power of that man's devices. I am not now obliged to hide myself in corners for fear of him. One of his intimate companions is become my warm friend, and engages to keep him from me, and that by his own consent. I am among honest people. I have all my clothes and effects restored to me. The wretch himself bears testimony to my honour (VII, 301).

The setting is never particularized to any extent. It originally represents the quality of safe harbor that Clarissa expresses above; later it draws its significance from the activities of Clarissa herself. It is, in fact, a curiously less "real" location than either Harlowe Place or the Sinclair lodging. But this is appropriate, for Clarissa here prepares to shed the real. From her arrival until her death, Clarissa is primarily engaged in two parallel activities, divesting herself of the physical world and preparing her move to another "house." Shortly after her arrival, for example, she requests that some of her rich clothing be sold:

> Her reason for so doing, she told them, was that she should never live to wear them: that her sister, and other relations, were above wearing them: that her mother would not endure in her sight any-thing that was hers: that she wanted the money: that she would be not be obliged to anybody, when she had effects by her for which she had no occasion (VI, 288).

Periodically in the weeks that follow she releases her laces and her fine dresses. She consigns her packets of letters; she names Belford as her executor to follow through on the final dispersement of her material property. This process of exfoliation comes to represent the final, more difficult abandonment of the physical: "Yet how this *body* clings! How it encumbers!" (VII, 278). Thus, in the Smith household, Clarissa almost ritualistically disengages herself from the concerns of the flesh and fastens her attention on the concerns of the spirit.

Her parallel activity, preparing her move to another house, is also conducted both on the literal and the symbolic level. She uses the words of Job to explain to Anna the comfort she feels in the approach of death: "God will soon *dissolve my substance; and bring me to death, and to the house appointed for all living*" (VII, 34). She employs the same metaphor in her allegorical letter to Lovelace, "I am setting out with all diligence for my father's house" (VII, 226). Lovelace's literal interpretation of the message serves to emphasize the almost supernatural control Clarissa has assumed over her own life. Her coffin comes to be the literal house she seeks ("As to what I want the money for — don't be surprised: — but suppose I want it to purchase a house?" [VII, 254]) — and it becomes the most hospitable house she has entered, for it is one that stands waiting ("near the window, like a harpsichord, though covered over to the ground" [VIII, 14]) without threat to integrity, without menace to her body, with only release for her spirit. In astounding patterns of irony, Clarissa dies — divested of all space and clothed in all space. The space intervening between life and death foreshortens and expands. The tiny confined space of her coffin opens to freedom. The house of her last weeks of earthly life is transmuted into the spiritual house of her death. And on the coffin is an inscription from Psalms:

> The days of man are but as grass. For he flourisheth as a flower of the field; for, as soon as the wind goeth over it, it is gone; and the place thereof shall know it no more.

VII. Conclusion

Although I have discussed time and space separately, they actually blend together in *Clarissa* as part of a unified dramatic development. *Clarissa* is a remarkable example of a novel in which not only the characters but also their spatial environments are presented in an imaginative world of time. Consequently, the spatial units, like the characters, show a progressive, interdependent change as the novel moves to its conclusion. By contrast, Grandison Hall and Mr. B.'s Lincolnshire estate are the units of qualified space in which the characters move; but these locations do not partake of the organic fusion that binds together the places, characters, and action of *Clarissa* into an unerring temporal journey. Thus, if later novelists turned to *Clarissa*, they found, in Richardson's treatment of space and time, their model for the novel of the relentlessness of man's internal experience in a physical world of time.

In tracing Richardson's treatment of time and space, we can observe a manifestation of what became probably the most persistent struggle in the development of the novel and of what still becomes a struggle with each novel that is written — the struggle to create a narrative that convincingly portrays the uniqueness of its characters and their environment, at the same time that it embodies a universality of application. Somewhere between the truth of his vision and the evanescence of his materials, the novelist must struggle to find the method that will allow him to realize both equally. We cannot know what conscious consideration Richardson gave to this struggle. Perhaps because he worked before theories of the novel became fashionable, and hence was free to follow his hunches; perhaps because he was caught between two artistic traditions with divergent ways of regarding the world; perhaps because he accidentally could do things he did not understand; his successes, particularly in *Clarissa*, reveal the struggle to make his form meaningfully deal with the dual problem of the unique and the universal. Thus, in his handling of time and space, we see Richardson exploring and often succeeding with problems that were to become generic principles of the novel.

Contemporary readers are not likely to accept Richardson with the enthusiasm that he generated in his first audience. Critics and literary historians are not likely to grant him a greater share of hierarchical honor than he now holds. But no one whose deepest literary commitments are with the novel can afford to dismiss him with a cliche. We know that the English novel could have developed without Richardson's middle-class, Puritan didacticism. Would it have been the same without his novelistic temperament?

THE MONOGRAPH SERIES

Vol. I,   No. 1   N. A. Pedersen   O.P.*
Everyman and Other Essays

           2   Milton R. Merrill
Reed Smoot: Utah Politician   O.P.

           3   Joel E. Ricks
Beginnings of Settlement in Cache Valley   O.P.
(Faculty Research Lecture No. 12)

           4   *Abstracts of Theses*   O.P.
1953 Commencement

Vol. II,   No. 1   Gwendella Thornley
How Beautiful Upon the Mountains   O.P.

           2   Leonard J. Arrington
*Orderville, Utah: A Pioneer Mormon Experiment in
Economic Organization*   O.P.

           3   Eldon J. Gardner
Genetics of Cancer and Other Abnormal Growths
(Faculty Research Lecture No. 13)

           4   *Abstracts of Theses*   O.P.
1954 Commencement

Vol. III,   No. 1   Marion L. Nielsen
Denmark's Johannes V. Jensen

           2   Ernest A. Jacobsen
Obligations of Higher Education to the Social Order
(Faculty Research Lecture No. 14)

           3   *Abstracts of Theses*
1955 Commencement

Vol. IV,   No. 1   M. Judd Harmon
The New Deal: A Revolution Consummated

           2   Delbert A. Greenwood
*Some Effects of Inorganic Fluoride on Plants,
Animals, and Man*   O.P.
(Faculty Research Lecture No. 15)

-----

* Out of print

3   Milton R. Merrill
    The Political Process   O.P.
    (Faculty Research Lecture No. 16)

4   *Abstracts of Theses*
    1956 Commencement

Vol. V,   No. 1   C. Wayne Cook
    *Range Livestock Nutrition and Its Importance
    in the Intermountain Region*
    (Faculty Research Lecture No. 17)

2   Maxwell D. Edwards
    The Tudors and the Church, 1509-1553

3   Evan B. Murray
    Some Economic Fallacies and the Citizen   O.P.
    (Faculty Honor Lecture No. 18)

4   *Abstracts of Theses*
    1957 Commencement

Vol. VI,   No. 1   J. Golden Taylor
    Neighbor Thoreau's Critical Humor   O.P.

2   Wayne D. Criddle
    Utah's Future Water Problems
    (Faculty Honor Lecture No. 19)

3   *Abstracts of Theses*
    1958 Commencement

Vol. VII, No. 1   Veneta Nielsen
    Under Sound   O.P.

2   Carlton F. Culmsee
    Malign Nature and the Frontier

3   Arthur H. Frietzsche
    The Monstrous Clever Young Man

4   Aldyth Thain
    Andre Gide's The Return of the Prodigal Son
    English Translation and Genesis

5   John M. Patrick
    Milton's Conception of Sin as Developed in Paradise Lost